One day Bean was on the grass. He saw a thrush. It landed in a bush.

Bean crept to the bush.

He looked up.

He saw the thrush on a branch next to a nest.

Bean jumped on to a branch. He looked up. The thrush had gone, but Bean saw the nest.

Bean jumped to the next branch to look in the nest.

The branch wobbled.

Bean wobbled, but he held on.

Then some moss, dust and twigs fell from the nest.

They fell on Bean.

The dust went in his eyes.

The branch wobbled again.

Then the nest fell on Bean, and he fell off the branch.

Bean landed on the grass. He had twigs, moss and dust all over him. He blinked to get the dust from his eyes.

He looked up to see Jelly and two eggshells on the grass next to him. "Bad Bean," she said. "You have had two eggs again."